ALIEN ENCOUNTERS
EXPOSED!

by Megan Cooley Peterson

CAPSTONE PRESS
a capstone imprint

Published by Spark, an imprint of Capstone
1710 Roe Crest Drive, North Mankato, Minnesota 56003
capstonepub.com

Library of Congress Cataloging-in-Publication Data is available on the Library of
Congress website.

ISBN: 9781666357059 (hardcover)
ISBN: 9781666357066 (ebook PDF)

Summary: Readers will be captivated by exciting tales of alien encounters while also
learning the facts about each claim.

Editorial Credits
Editor: Mandy Robbins; Designer: Heidi Thompson; Media Researchers: Jo Miller
and Pam Mitsakos; Production Specialist: Tori Abraham

Image Credits
Alamy: Carver Mostardi, 23, Chronicle, 8, Kiyoshi Takahase Segundo, 25;
Getty Images: Bettmann, 12, gremlin, 26, simonbradfield, 11; Shutterstock:
AlbertoGonzalez, 15, CrackerClips Stock Media, 21, DanieleGay, 5, Joeprachatree,
29, petrmalinak, 7, Raggedstone, Cover, 2, solarseven, 17; Superstock: The Science
Picture Company, 18

All internet sites appearing in back matter were available and accurate when this
book was sent to press.

TABLE OF CONTENTS

Out of this World!....................4

Visitor from Venus...................6

The Betty and Barney Hill Case......10

Taken in the Woods..................14

Caught on Tape......................20

Aliens Down Under...................24

Glossary.................... 30

Read More................... 31

Internet Sites............. 31

Index...................... 32

About the Author........... 32

Words in **bold** are in the glossary.

OUT OF THIS WORLD!

Visitors from outer space. Little green men. Space aliens have amazed humans for ages. But are they real? Some people say they have met them. Many **encounters** have been proven false. But not all of them have. Read on and decide for yourself.

VISITOR FROM VENUS

For years, George Adamski took pictures of **UFOs**. He wondered if aliens were real. In 1952, George and his friends were in a California desert. Suddenly, a bell-shaped craft landed nearby.

George moved toward the craft. An alien waved. George said it looked human. It stood about 5 feet tall.

George Adamski and Desmond Leslie wrote the book *Flying Saucers Have Landed*.

The alien told George it was from Venus. It had a message for the people of Earth. It told them to stop using bombs. Then the alien got back in its ship and flew away.

Many people didn't believe George's tale. But his friends said they saw it too. George never changed his story.

THE BETTY AND BARNEY HILL CASE

In September 1961, Betty and Barney Hill were driving home one night. They saw an odd light in the sky. It followed them. They stopped to look at it. But they didn't remember what happened next. Hours later, they found themselves at home.

FACT

Betty and Barney's watches stopped working on the drive home.

Betty and Barney Hill

The Hills later remembered what happened. They said gray aliens with huge eyes took them into a spaceship. The aliens studied them and then erased their memories.

This case is hard to prove. There were no witnesses. Many people believed the Hills were just overtired. They could have seen things that weren't there. The Hills insisted that wasn't what happened.

TAKEN IN THE WOODS

In 1975, Travis Walton worked as a logger. On November 5, he and some fellow workers were driving through the woods near Heber, Arizona. The men saw a strange light. They drove toward it. They discovered a UFO.

Travis got out of the truck to check it out. The craft hung in the air. It was about 20 feet long. It was shaped like a disc.

Suddenly, a bright light zapped Travis! The other men drove off, afraid. When they came back, Travis was gone. They told the police what they had seen. But no one could find Travis.

Travis showed up five days later. He said the light had pulled him onto the craft. Three short, human-like aliens put him on a table. He had trouble breathing. Soon, he passed out. He woke up lying near a highway.

FACT

Travis took lie detector tests about his experience. He passed some and failed others.

CAUGHT ON TAPE

In 1995, a grainy video shocked the world. It showed U.S. government workers looking at something. They wore safety suits and gloves. What were they studying? An alien! The video **claimed** the alien had been found in Roswell, New Mexico, in 1947.

> **FACT**
> In 1947, a farmer found a strange object near Roswell, New Mexico. He thought it might be an alien spacecraft.

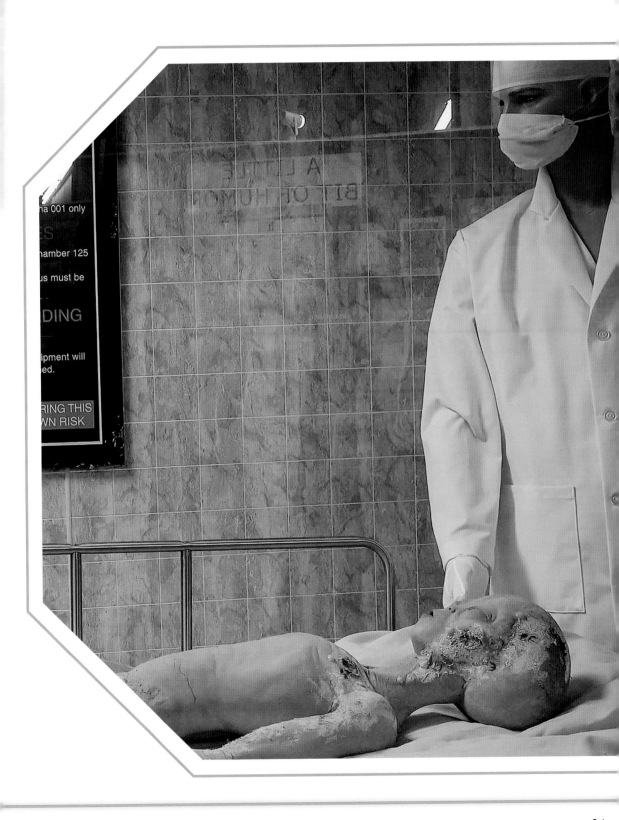

21

Special effects artist John Humphreys later said the video was a fake. He made the alien creature. Two friends helped him make the video. They said it was based on a real alien caught on film. That film has never been found.

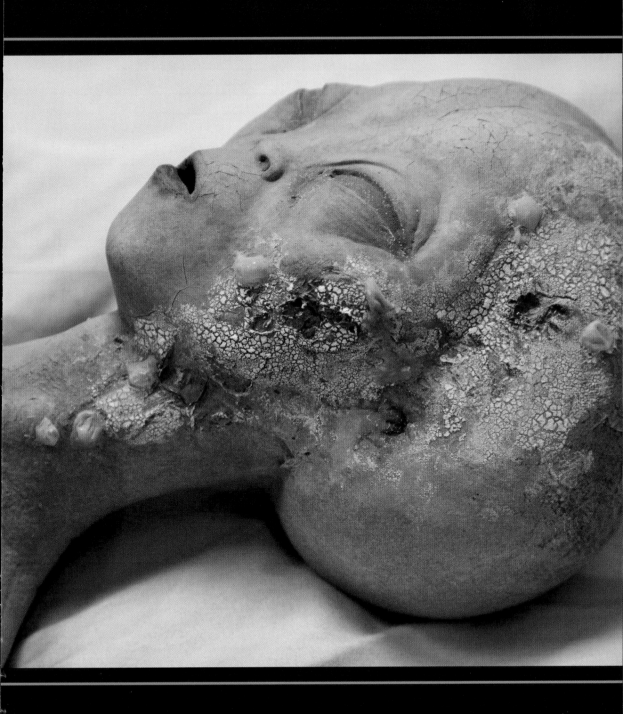

ALIENS
DOWN UNDER

It was a dark night in 1993. Kelly and Andrew Cahill were driving home near Melbourne, Australia. They saw strange orange lights up ahead. The lights floated in the sky.

Kelly looked closer. The lights were windows. It was a spacecraft! Creatures moved about inside. Then the craft flew away.

The craft landed in a field. Kelly and Andrew stopped to look at it. It looked like a **blimp**. Several thin creatures with red eyes climbed out. They sent out a blast of energy. It hit Kelly in the stomach. She couldn't remember anything else that happened that night.

Kelly's odd experiences continued. Her stomach hurt. She found a **wound** there. It was shaped like a triangle. She even said the aliens visited her at night.

Kelly found researchers who studied alien encounters. The researchers met others who had seen the aliens that night. Some said they were taken aboard. Did it really happen? You decide!

FACT

Kelly wrote a book about her experience called *Encounter*.

Glossary

blimp (BLIMP)—an airship without a rigid frame, much like a balloon

claim (KLAYM)—to say that something is true

encounter (en-KOUN-tur)—an unexpected or difficult meeting

special effect (SPESH-uhl uh-FEKT)—an illusion created for movies or TV using special props, camera systems, computer graphics, and other methods

UFO (YOO EF OH)—an object in the sky thought to be a spaceship from another planet; UFO is short for unidentified flying object

wound (WOOND)—an injury or cut

Read More

Chanez, Katie. *Alien Abductions.* North Mankato, MN: Capstone Press, 2020.

Croy, Anita. *Taken from the Forest: An Alien Abduction.* Minneapolis: Bearport Publishing Company, 2022.

Olson, Gillia M. *Curious About Aliens.* Mankato, MN: Amicus, 2022.

Internet Sites

Are Aliens Real?
kidscoop.com/this-week-in-kid-scoop/are-aliens-real/

NASA Kids' Club
nasa.gov/kidsclub/index.html

Science with Sam: Do Aliens Exist?
newscientist.com/article/2274302-science-with-sam-do-aliens-exist/

Index

Adamski, George, 6, 7, 8, 9

Cahill, Kelly and Andrew, 24, 27, 28

Hill, Betty and Barney, 10, 12, 13
Humphreys, John, 22

Roswell, New Mexico, 20

UFOs, 6, 7, 10, 13, 14, 16, 19, 20, 24, 27
U.S. government, 20

Venus, 9

Walton, Travis, 14, 16, 19

About the Author

Megan Cooley Peterson has been an avid reader and writer since she was a little girl. She has written nonfiction children's books about topics ranging from urban legends to gross animal facts. She lives in Minnesota with her husband, daughter, and cuddly kitty.